For Odette

D0549727

FLOWER SHOP
Secrets

BY SALLY PAGE

FANAHAN BOOKS

Text copyright © Sally Page 2008
Photography copyright © Sally Page 2008
Design & Layout copyright © Billy Kelly 2008

First published in 2008
Printed and bound in China by C&C Offset Printing

Also by Sally Page:
The Flower Shop - A Year in the Life of an English Country Flower Shop
The Flower Shop Christmas
and
Flower Shops & Friends

All rights reserved. No part of this publication may be reproduced in any material
form (including photocopying or storing it in any medium by electronic means and
whether or not transiently or incidentally to some other use of this publication)
without written permission of the copyright owner, except in accordance with the
provisions of the Copyright, Designs and Patents Act 1988 or under the terms of a
licence issued by the Copyright Licensing Agency,
90 Tottenham Court Road, London W1P 9HE.

A CIP catalogue record for this book is available from the British Library

ISBN: 978-0-9553779-3-8

For sales contact:
The Manning Partnership
6 The Old Dairy,
Melcombe Road,
Bath, BA2 3LR.
Telephone 0044 (0) 1225 478444
Fax 0044 (0) 1225 478440
E-mail sales@manning-partnership.co.uk
Distribution: Grantham Book Services

Published by Fanahan Books
Evelyn House, Leddington Way, Gillingham, Dorset, SP8 4FF
www.englishflowershop.com

Contents

Introduction

This book brings together the Flower Shop Secrets that feature in my first three flower books, as I thought that the collection might make a useful and pretty guide for readers.

Working as a florist in a beautiful village flower shop I have seen how much our customers seem to enjoy the florist tips and hints that we pass on to them. So when it came to photographing and writing books about flower shops I thought it would be a good idea to include these tricks of the trade to help other flower-lovers. I stuck to the ideas that I know from experience really work and I avoided tasks that were time consuming and complicated – if I knew I wouldn't really be bothered to do something I did not suggest it to others!

The hints that I compiled included gathering Flower Shop Secrets from the talented florists I met on my journey around English flower shops – a year spent visiting some of the most beautiful parts of England and eavesdropping on the lives of the flower shops I discovered there. So I would also like thank these florists for their help and enthusiasm.

FLOWER SHOP
Essentials

These 'Flower Shop Essentials' illustrate some of the most important and yet easy rules to follow to ensure your flowers last as long as possible. I have also included some simple arranging tips to help you get the most out of your flowers.

CONDITIONING

Always, always, re-cut your flowers before you put them in water. It may only take stems a few minutes out in the air to seal over, making it difficult for the flowers to drink. Cut them at an angle and you will ensure that they can drink as much as possible as the stems will not be resting flush against the bottom of the vase.

Flowers like their vase water to be luke-warm rather than ice cold.

flower shop secrets
CARRYING FLOWERS

If you are taking flowers on a long journey, choose a compact hand-tied bouquet with an aqua-pack. This can then be fitted into a straight-sided carrier bag which will help protect the flowers.

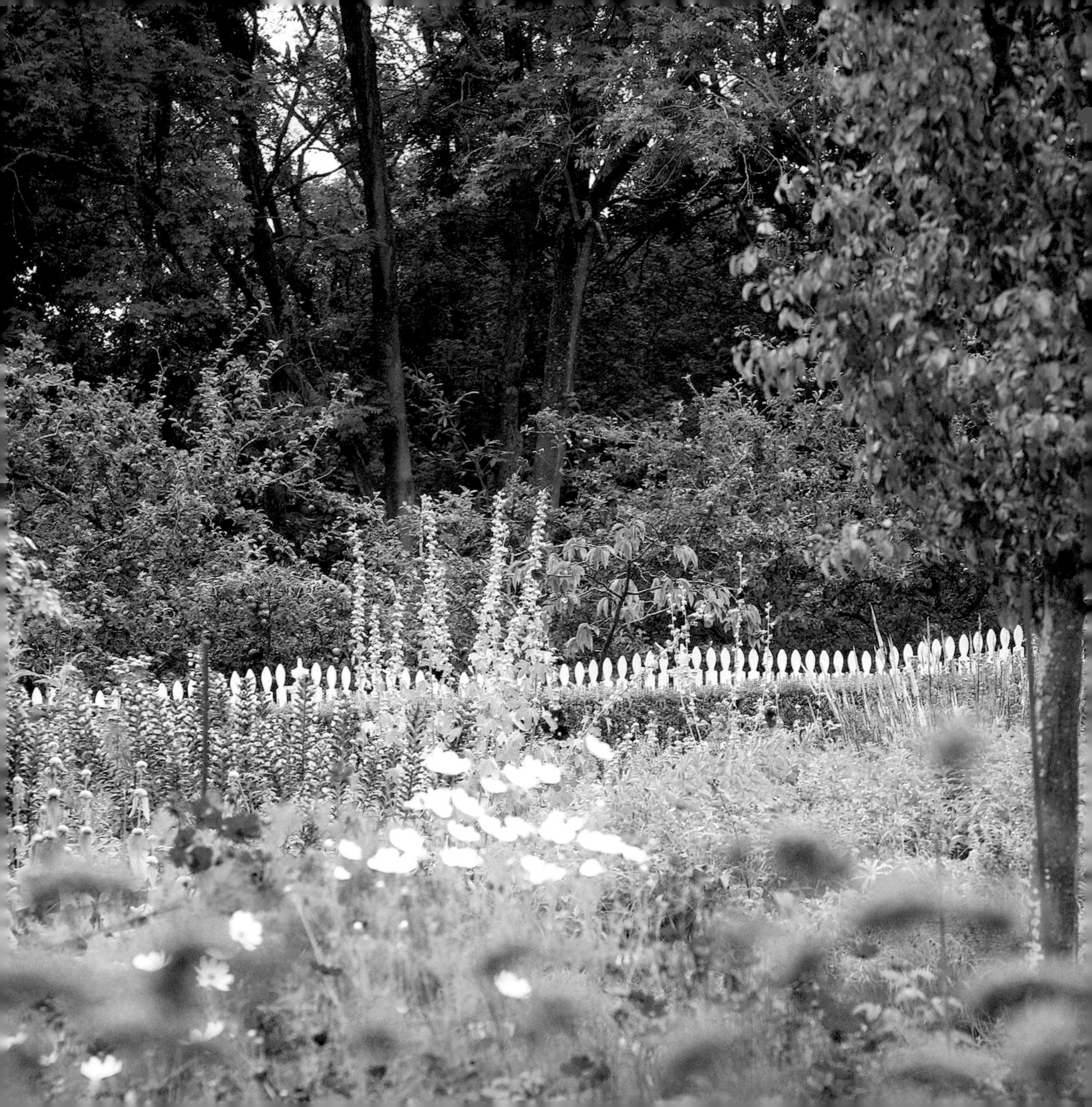

flower shop secrets

FLOWER CARE

To help flowers last longer strip the lower leaves off so they are not immersed in water. This helps prevent bacteria forming. For the same reason it is also important not to bash or hammer the ends of flower stems.

flower shop secrets
FIVE ESSENTIAL VASES

If I could only have five vases at home these are the ones I would choose, left to right, the medium vase, the bud vase, the posy vase, the mini 'goldfish' bowl and the tall slim vase. They look right in the places I want to position flowers and they are suitable for most of the flowers I am likely to use. They will cover the majority of occasions and, very importantly, they do not need hundreds of flowers in them to look good.

flower shop secrets
GLASS

If glass vases have crusty water stains that cannot be washed off we fill the vases with water and drop in one or two Steradent tablets and leave them overnight. In the morning the stains are easy to wash away.

Rachel Lilley's beautiful flower shop in Walcot Street, Bath

FRIDGES AND FRUIT

Flowers quite like the cold which is why florists store buttonholes and corsages in the fridge. And flowers will also last longer if they are put somewhere cooler at night – such as on a windowsill or in a back porch. However flowers do not like to be near fruit so if you are looking for a cool spot for your vase of flowers try not to stand them by the fruit bowl.

flower shop secrets

COLOUR

Many people struggle to decide which flowers they should put together for a gift, so if people are unsure we often suggest sticking to one kind of flower or recommend choosing flowers that are all the same type of colour. One combination that always looks good is to mix white and cream flowers together with interesting foliage.

flower shop secrets

CONTAINERS

This may seem obvious, but you can always put a watertight pot inside a fragile and more attractive container. In the shop we are often looking for new ways to display the flowers and may well grab a chipped vase or battered pot, wedge it in a beautiful basket or terracotta pot, and then fill it with flowers without bothering to line the container or get the Oasis out.

flower shop secrets

THREE BUNCHES OF FLOWERS

To see the different looks that can be achieved with the same flowers, we arrange a similar bunch of flowers in three different ways. We base the bunch on nine stems: purple larkspur, lilac stock, and creamy lisianthus. It is easier to get a balanced and pleasing effect with an odd number of flowers, so we often build up arrangements using 3, 5, or 7 stems of one flower type. Of course this rule goes out the window if someone sends you a dozen roses. By arranging each flower type at a different height in the container you give your arrangement depth and interest.

PARTY FLOWERS

For an easy and striking flower arrangement crinkle cellophane into a tall glass vase, fill with water and then add a hand-tied arrangement to the top. Flower heads can be placed in amongst the cellophane for extra effect.

Another easy, yet impressive arrangement is to place an Oasis ring inside a twig wreath with a hurricane lamp in the centre. Cut hyacinths can then be arranged into the Oasis base.

Sometimes customers bring in containers they would like us to re-use, including the Oasis that is inside. We are always happy to use the container but would never re-use the Oasis as the previously formed holes and indentations can create air holes that stop the new flowers from drinking. For the same reason, when working with new Oasis you need to be careful not to push the stems in too far so they have to be withdrawn as you adjust them.

To help arrange flowers in a square container tie crisscross bands of ribbons around the vase.

FLOWER SHOP
Favourites

flower shop secrets
HYACINTH

When you trim the bottom of a hyacinth leave as much of the bulbous stem attached as you can, something within this part of the plant helps the hyacinth stay strong and straight. And as the fragrance of a hyacinth gets stronger the older it gets be careful not to throw them away too soon.

Hyacinths are poisonous and it is quite common to end up with a rash on your hands and face if you are not careful when handling them.

Hyacinth meaning: Playful

flower shop secrets
ANEMONE

Flowers with hairy stems, such as anemones do not like to stand in deep water, they are much happier if just the bottom part of their stem is covered.

Anemone meaning: Forsaken

flower shop secrets

TULIP

If we have more tulips than we need in our delivery from market we store them at the back of the shop out of water for later. They do not mind this in the least. It also means this is a good flower to take to someone if you know they have to be out of water for a while. If you don't want your tulips to get droopy, which they can do as they grow so fast in water, prick their stems with a pin just under the head and they will keep standing upright.

Tulip meaning: Beautiful eyes

Alstroemeria meaning: Aspiring

flower shop secrets
ALSTROEMERIA

The leaves of the alstroemeria tend to flop and die well before the flowers do, so make sure you remove the leaves if you are using them in an arrangement.

flower shop secrets
LISIANTHUS

Lisianthus flowers don't like to be splashed with water as water spots can make their petals go mouldy.

Lisianthus meaning: Calming

flower shop secrets

PEONY

If your peony heads are very tight and they do not look like they will open, rinse the heads in cold water as this can help release the petals.

Peony meaning: Most beautiful

ROSE

If your roses get floppy, wrap their heads in paper so they are held upright, re-cut the stems and stand them in very hot water. Leave them there overnight and if they can be revived they will be by the morning.

Pink rose meaning: Friendship

Red rose meaning: Passionate love

flower shop secrets
LILY

Lilies last longer if the pollen is removed as this tricks the flower into thinking it must bloom for longer. Use a tissue to pinch off the pollen, but be careful not to get it on your clothes as it stains. If you do get lily pollen on your clothes do not try to brush it off or remove it with water, this only makes things worse. Instead, use Sellotape to remove the pollen by gently dabbing it.

Lily meaning: Celebration

flower shop secrets
DELPHINIUM

If delphiniums do break you can cut them down and fill a smaller vase with pieces of the stem for a more compact display.

Delphinium meaning: Boldness

flower shop secrets
SWEET PEA

I must admit I don't have a secret for sweet peas, but I love them so much I couldn't resist including them here. They are a delicate flower which will only really last for a few days when cut. However, the good news is, the more you cut them, the more they flower.

Sweet Pea meaning: Shyness

flower shop secrets
FREESIA

Customers often choose freesias because of their wonderful fragrance. However, not all varieties of freesias are heavily scented, for example, some white freesias hardly smell at all. If you love the scent of freesias the pink and red varieties tend to be the most heavily perfumed.

Freesia meaning: Spirited

Orchid meaning: Delicate beauty

flower shop secrets
ORCHID

Orchid plants do not like to be over-watered, however a stem of orchids will look wonderful and be very happy fully submerged in a tall glass vase full of water.

flower shop secrets
HYDRANGEA

Hydrangeas make a wonderful display on their own in a large vase or jug, but if you find they are too big for your room you can always take just one and tuck other flowers and foliage in amongst the petals for a smaller posy.

Hydrangea meaning: Perserverance

Amaryllis meaning: Pride

flower shop secrets

AMARYLLIS

Some amaryllis heads can be so heavy once the flowers are open that they are in danger of snapping or bending the stem. If you think this may happen put a stick up the hollow tube of the stem to give additional hidden support.

FLOWER SHOP
Friends

For my third book I spent a year traveling around England searching out beautiful flower shops and talented florists. These are the flower shop secrets they were kind enough to share with me.

Picture over: All the florists I discover on my journey join me in the Cotswolds for a Florists' Lunch

56

As a rule of thumb, the longer the stem, the fatter the head of the rose. So when you pay more for a long stemmed rose do not be afraid to cut it down if you want to. You are not wasting money by discarding the stem, your money has also been spent on the larger bloom.

Ted Martin Flowers,
Tisbury, Wiltshire

flower shop secrets
THE FLOWER BOUTIQUE

Florists always tell customers how important it is to re-cut flowers when they get them home because it takes no time at all for the stems to seal over, making it difficult for the flowers to drink. However, there are certain spring flowers that are exceptions to this rule. The sap of daffodils and narcissi are poisonous to other flowers so we recommend you do not re-cut their stems if you intend to mix them with other varieties.

the flower boutique, Linton, Cambridgeshire

flower shop secrets
VAAS

When considering putting a palette of flowers together think of the flowers as having different personalities, so in the same way as you would not mix certain people together do not mix certain flowers. For example, you would not sit a very robust flower next to a timid flower. Thinking about the flowers in this way it is quite easy to know what mix of personalities should go in a bouquet or in an arrangement.

Vaas, Hockley, Nottingham

flower shop secrets

MISS PICKERING

To keep vase water free from the bacteria that can reduce the life of flowers and cause the stems to become slimy and smelly, add half a Steritab or other such water purification tablet to the water with the flowers.

Miss Pickering, Stamford, Lincolnshire

flower shop secrets

RACHEL LILLEY

With their bendy stems and attractive, pliable leaves, tulips are happy to be curved around the inside of a bowl to create a stylish but very easy table centre. It is important to keep an eye on the water level in the bowl as tulips are thirsty flowers and will drain it very quickly.

Rachel Lilley, Walcot Street, Bath

flower shop secrets
BLUE

Treat flowers well and they will last longer. The way for conditioning gerberas is a good example of this. When the gerberas arrive from market cut the stems making sure their heads are supported and let them have a good drink. This could be for up to twelve hours. As the stems are upright and they are not taking the weight of the flower-heads this enables them to become firm and strong.

blue, Shifnal, Shropshire.

flower shop secrets
WHITE GDN

When working with woody stemmed flowers, such as hydrangeas, cut the stems into a 'V' shape at the base (rather than the slanting cut we would normally suggest). This gives a greater surface area for the water to be drawn up the stem and helps pierce the Oasis if you are using the flowers in an arrangement.

White Gdn, Henley on Thames, Oxfordshire

Smith Street Deli, Dartmouth, Devon

flower shop secrets

SMITH STREET DELI

Crystallised rose petals are pretty, edible and decorative. They can also be added to Champagne, rather than a sugar cube, when making a Champagne cocktail. Use roses that have not been sprayed with any pesticides, wash the petals and remove the white bit at the base (this has a bitter taste). Dissolve a quarter of a tablespoon of gum arabic in a tablespoon of water and brush this on the petals. Sprinkle the petals with caster sugar and leave on baking paper to dry.

flower shop secrets
POTTING SHED FLORIST

Why only have a wreath on your door at Christmas time? Hang a twig heart wreath on your front door all year round and then add seasonal things to the basic wreath as the seasons change, such as fresh lavender from the garden or berries and fruit in the autumn.

Potting Shed Florist, Navenby, Lincolnshire

flower shop secrets

GREEN PAVILLION

For a stylish but quick table arrangement put about three inches of water in a goldfish bowl and twist some contorted hazel around the inside of the bowl. Then place chrysanthum blooms, cut very short, in the bottom of the vase.

Another tip for autumn: take a glass vase and then place a smaller vase inside it. Fill the space in between with conkers and then place your flowers in the second vase.

Green Pavilion, Buxton, Derbyshire

THE FLOWER SHOP

After carving out part of a pumpkin, fill the hole with soaked Oasis. This can then be used as the base for a seasonal display of Calla lilies, protea and peach ilex. This also works well with other fruit and vegetables as their outer skins help to keep the Oasis moist.

The Flower Shop, Ambleside, Cumbria

flower shop secrets
CARL BANKS

When preparing potted amaryllis and hyacinths cover the compost around the plants with moss. When Christmas is approaching place ilex or hawthorne berries amongst the moss to give a seasonal twist to the pots.

Carl Banks, Yarm, North Yorkshire

The bottoms of Amaryllis stems often split and curl up making it difficult to fit them into the bottom of the vase. Slip a rubber band around the end of each stem to stop this happening.

Spriggs, Petworth, Sussex

FLOWER SHOP
Christmas

flower shop secrets
BERRIES

In some years holly bushes are laden with berries, but in years when they are scarce we use artificial berries wired around the holly sprigs. If the rest of the arrangement is full and natural no one notices that these berries are not real. Another attractive alternative to holly berries is scarlet rosehips.

flower shop secrets
TABLE CENTRES

If you don't have time to make a table decoration take a door wreath and place it in the centre of the table with a church candle in the middle.

flower shop secrets
GARLANDS

Some customers like to buy plain garlands which they then decorate themselves. Sprigs of ivy, hypericum and holly can be wired into the pine, although always leave the holly until last, otherwise you will get pricked as you wire other things in. Ribbon, pine cones, slices of dried fruit and bundles of cinnamon sticks also work well. Garlands dry out very quickly over a fireplace so an alternative is to line up a number of arrangements so they look like a garland. In this case five large zinc containers are filled with Oasis and ivy and then strung with Christmas lights and hung with stars.

flower shop secrets

DRIED ORANGES

I have tried many different ways to dry orange slices but I have found the best method is to place them on a cake rack on top of the Aga. The second best is in a fan assisted oven on a very low heat.

MISTLETOE

Take some mistletoe berries and rub them into the fork of a tree in your garden. This imitates the action of a Mistle Thrush and may well be the beginning of your own mistletoe crop.

flower shop secrets

TEST TUBES

Test tubes filled with water are really useful if you wish to hang flowers amongst greenery and keep them fresh. They are also good for thick-stemmed flowers, like hyacinths, that can be tricky to push into Oasis. Sometimes it is easier to place a few test tubes into the Oasis and then add the flowers to the tubes.

flower shop secrets
FESTIVE VASES

At Christmas time I fill the vases I am not using for flowers with all sorts of festive decorations – such as candles surrounded by pine cones or the extra baubles I can't fit on the Christmas tree.

Also in The Flower Shop series:

The Flower Shop
A year in the life of an English Country Flower Shop

The Flower Shop Christmas
Christmas in an English Country Flower Shop

Flower Shops & Friends
A year's journey around English Flower Shops

For full details visit:
www.englishflowershop.com

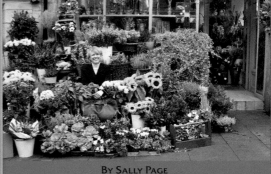